OCEAN LIFE

Brenda Z. Guiberson

SCHOLASTIC
REFERENCE

PHOTO CREDITS: COVER: Bruce Coleman Inc., New York. **Bruce Coleman Inc.** : 5: Larry Lipsky; 6–7: Tom Brakefield; 9, 10: Ron & Valerie Taylor; 15: John Hyde; 20: Joe McDonald; 25, 32: Tui De Roy; 37: Ron & Valerie Taylor; 39: Mark Jones; 40–41: Tui De Roy. **Dembinsky Photo Associates**, Oswosso, MI: 12, 27: Bill Curtsinger. Courtesy of **Brenda Guiberson**: 2. **NASA**: 3. **Peter Arnold, Inc.**, New York: 1: Jeffrey L. Rotman; 16–17: Mark Carwardine; 26: Norbert Wu. **Photo Researchers**, New York: 8: Mary Beth Angelo; 13: Meckes; 18, 19: Francois Gohier; 21: Steinhart Aquarium; 22–23: Richard Ellis; 24: Bud Lehnhausen; 28: Francois Gohier; 29: Barry Lopez; 31: Tim Davis; 33, 34, 36: Francois Gohier; 43: Bill Bachman; 44–45: Gregory Ochocki.

Library of Congress Cataloging-in-Publication Data available.

ISBN 0-439-31632-4

Book design by Barbara Balch and Kay Petronio
Photo research by Sarah Longacre

13 12 11 10 9   13 14 15 16 17/0

Printed in the U.S.A.   40

First trade printing, March 2002

We are grateful to Francie Alexander, reading specialist, and to
Adele M. Brodkin, Ph.D., developmental psychologist, for their
contributions to the development of this series.

Our thanks also to our science consultants: Dr. Vincent F. Gallucci,
Professor, School of Fisheries, University of Washington, and Lisa Mielke,
Assistant Director of Education, Aquarium for Wildlife Conservation, Brooklyn, New York.

Author Brenda Z. Guiberson
with a dolphin in Hawaii.

Seventy percent of our planet is covered by oceans. The water floods over volcanoes, mountains, trenches, and plains on the ocean floor. The ocean can be very deep, as much as 35,000 feet (10,500 meters). Because sunlight does not reach below 3,300 feet (1,000 meters), the ocean can also be totally dark.

Strange and amazing creatures live in the ocean. Some are fish, others are not. Some are huge, others are tiny. Some have thousands of teeth, others have none.

But all of these creatures have two things in common: They need to breathe oxygen and to eat.

A tiger shark zigzags as he swims in the ocean. He is a huge fish, 14 feet (4.2 meters) long. His tail swings from side to side to push him through the water.

Like all fish, he breathes when
water flows over his **gills**. The gills
absorb oxygen from the water and
move it into the bloodstream of
the fish.

Lice, small crab-like creatures, live in the soft gills of the shark. The lice nibble and nip. The tiger shark wants to get rid of them, so he swims to a nearby coral reef for a cleaning! The shark stays very still while coral shrimp eat the lice. He even stops breathing for a time so the shrimp can climb far into his gill slits to get a good meal.

Take a Closer Look

Close-up of a coral shrimp

The shark and lice live together
in a relationship called parasitism
(**pa**-ruh-sit-iz-uhm). The lice are
parasites that eat shark tissue. There
is no benefit for the shark, and too
many parasites could harm the shark.

The shark–coral shrimp
relationship is called mutualism
(**myoo**-choo-uhl-iz-uhm). Both
creatures benefit from each other.

When the tiger shark is hungry,
he will eat almost anything—a
turtle, an octopus, even an old shoe.
But he does not try to eat the quick
little fish that swim with him. These
fish, called pilot fish, are too hard
to catch.

The tiger shark smells a crab. He has a good nose and follows the scent. He can also detect tiny movements, sounds, and even the electrical field around the crab.

The tiger shark lunges with his eyes closed and jaws wide open. *CHOMP!* While he munches, the pilot fish dart in to eat the scraps.

The relationship between the shark and the pilot fish is called commensalism (kuh-**men**-suhl-iz-uhm). The fish get food scraps to eat, but there is no benefit or harm to the shark.

One of the tiger shark's teeth falls out and drifts down, down to the sandy bottom of the ocean. The shark does not miss it because he has rows and rows of extra teeth. When a tooth falls out, another takes its place. Each year, the tiger shark replaces about 1,500 teeth. If the shark lives 40 years, that's 60,000 lost teeth!

Close-up of a shark's denticles (artificially colored)

The tiger shark also has millions of tiny, tiny teeth that cover his skin. These skin-teeth are called denticles (**den**-ti-kuhlz). They make the shark's skin rough and tough like sandpaper. The denticles are surrounded by pits that are similar to taste buds. But scientists don't know for sure if sharks can taste.

More than 350 kinds of sharks live in the ocean. The smallest, the dwarf dogshark, was discovered in 1985. It is about as long as a pencil.

The gentle whale shark is the largest fish in the ocean. It can reach 45 feet (13.5 meters) in length.

Big or little, all sharks are fish. But they have no bones in their bodies. Shark skeletons are made of cartilage (**kar**-tuh-lij)—the flexible material found in your ears and nose.

◆ ◆ ◆

Farther out at sea, a blue whale glides through the ocean. She is not a fish with gills like the tiger shark. She is a mammal that breathes air. She swims to the surface to get the oxygen she needs.

PROOSH! She blows out air from the double blowholes on top of her head. The two blowholes are giant nostrils like the holes in your nose. As she breathes out old air, the puff rises 30 feet (9 meters) and smells like rotten fish.

The blue whale fills her lungs with fresh air. She blows again and again. Then she lifts her huge tail **flukes** to dive beneath the surface. Flukes are the two parts of a whale's tail. As a whale swims, strong muscles pull the flukes up and down to push the whale forward.

It is spring, and the blue whale has a baby. The baby likes to nuzzle against the smooth skin of his mother and nurse. Every day, the baby whale drinks 100 gallons (378 liters) of creamy milk. And every day, the baby gains 200 pounds (90 kilograms).

Baby blue whales grow fast. When they are full-grown, blue whales are the biggest animals on Earth. Some blue whales reach 100 feet (30 meters) in length—as long as three school buses. They can weigh 150 tons (152 tonnes), as much as twenty-five elephants.

Even though she is one of the largest animals in the sea, the blue whale eats only the smallest creatures in the ocean. She swims into a swarm of tiny pink shrimp called krill.

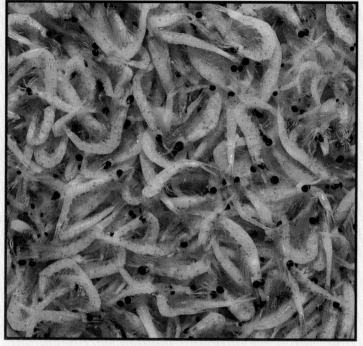

Close-up of krill

She opens her mouth, puffs out her throat like a balloon, and takes a big gulp. The whale sucks in enough water and krill to flood three rooms of a house.

21

The blue whale's tongue is the size of a speedboat, but there are no teeth in her mouth. Instead, plates of baleen (bay-**leen**) dangle from her upper jaw. The baleen is made of keratin (**ker**-uh-tin), a material like your fingernails. The plates look like bristles on a broom—packed together on top and frayed at the bottom.

After she takes in a huge mouthful of water and krill, the blue whale shoves the water out with her tongue. The krill get trapped in the baleen. The whale licks them off and swallows. She is a **filter feeder** who can eat 40 million krill in one day.

Blue whales can be very noisy. They make the loudest sound of any animal on the Earth—great moans that rumble across the ocean. Other blue whales hear these sounds for hundreds of miles (kilometers). But people can hear blue whale moans only with special equipment. The vibrations of these sound waves are too low-pitched to be detected by human ears.

Most creatures in the ocean do not bother blue whales. But a shark only several inches (centimeters) long likes to eat whale **blubber** and will even take a bite out of the biggest animal on Earth.

The little cookiecutter shark glows in the dark. If a blue whale comes near, the shark grabs on with her suction-cup lips. Then she spins like a top and cuts out a chunk of blubber to eat. The soft skin of the whale will heal, but the bite leaves a scar the size of a cookie.

The mouth of a cookiecutter shark

Cookiecutter shark scars have also been seen on other kinds of whales, sharks, tuna, and dolphins.

27

Not all the whales in the ocean are baleen whales. Some whales have teeth. A 60-foot (18-meter) sperm whale has teeth that can be as long as bananas. He also has skin that can be 14 inches (35 centimeters) thick, including blubber.

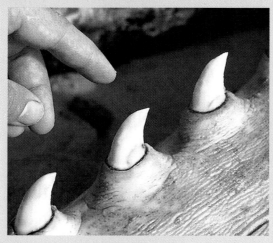

Sperm whales have teeth only on the lower jaw.

The sperm whale dives down, down into the deep, dark ocean. He stays underwater for an hour looking for food. No one knows exactly how the sperm whale hunts in the darkness, but the whale eats lots of squid, both small and large. Squid have eight arms, two long tentacles, and a sharp beak. Thousands of beaks, and even whole squid, have been found in the stomach of a single sperm whale. From this evidence we know that the sperm whale can find and eat the very large and mysterious giant squid.

There are many kinds of toothed whales in the ocean. Some have only two teeth. One tooth of the male narwhal keeps growing until it forms a tusk that can be 10 feet (3 meters) long.

There are also several kinds of baleen whales. The gray whale gulps mud from the ocean bottom and then filters out the food. The humpback whale can blow bubbles into a "bubble net" to trap food before taking a big gulp.

◆ ◆ ◆

The sperm whale comes up for
a blow near a pod of bottlenose
dolphins. The dolphins leap high and
spin. They breathe through single
blowholes without slowing down.
They are mammals like the whale,
but are much smaller. These adults are
about 10 feet (3 meters) long.

The dolphins dive underwater and whistle to one another. Every dolphin has a different whistle, as unique to that dolphin as your face is to you. A baby dolphin that is part of the pod practices his own whistle.

Then he finds his mother and nurses before he heads back to the surface to breathe. Someday he will be able to stay underwater for seven minutes like the adult dolphins do.

Bottlenose dolphins also make a clicking sound. The dolphins click fast—one hundred times a second—and wait for an echo to come back to them. This method, called **echolocation** (ek-oh-loh-**kay**-shuhn), is the way they find their food. When the sound bounces off a school of fish, the dolphins have located a feast.

They swim into the school and whip their tails through the water. The fish get confused and the dolphins can catch them easily.

The baby dolphin is ready for his first taste of fish. The mother bites off a fish head so the baby will not eat any big bones. He tosses the fish and plays with it before he finally swallows it in a gulp.

Now the dolphins work together to herd up a school of small squid. The dolphins grab squid with their teeth and swallow them without chewing. Far away, hammerhead sharks sense the action and smell the blood. The hammerheads swing their big heads back and forth as they come to eat.

There is some bumping and shoving as the dolphins scatter. The mother dolphin is stunned by a swinging shark tail. Two dolphins slide under her and nudge her to the surface to breathe. When she recovers, they swim away.

The hammerheads eat faster and faster. All the smells and movement in the water may be too much for them. They start to bite everything in sight.

As the teeth snap at anything that moves, a shark is injured and then quickly eaten by other sharks. This behavior is called a feeding frenzy.

The ocean is home to more than thirty different kinds of dolphins. All of them have teeth and are closely related to the toothed whales. The largest dolphin is the orca, which can reach 30 feet (9 meters) long. The small Commerson's dolphin is 5 feet (1.5 meters) long.

The dolphins are tired. The blue whale swims near them with her baby. As the whale moves through the ocean, she pushes along a huge wave of water. The dolphins swim in front of her and catch a restful ride. The pressure of the whale's **bow wave** lets the dolphins glide along easily, like body surfers.

The shimmering blue water hides many more wonderful creatures. The ocean is so deep and vast that it may contain the greatest number of living things on the planet.

As we build new diving machines, more will be discovered. Big or little, fish or not, an uncountable number of creatures find a home in the ocean.

Glossary

blubber—a layer of fat in the skin of whales and other sea mammals that keeps them warm in the cold ocean and also stores food

bow wave—a strong wave that gets pushed ahead of boats or whales (or other large creatures) as they move through the water

echolocation (ek-oh-loh-**kay**-shuhn)—the use of sound waves and their echoes to find objects

filter feeder—an ocean animal with special mouth parts that eats by filtering, or straining, tiny plants and animals out of the water

flukes—the powerful tail of a whale that moves up and down to push the whale through the water

gills—organs that allow fish to breathe oxygen from the water

Index

A Note to Parents

Learning to read is such an exciting time in a child's life. You may delight in sharing your favorite fairy tales and picture books with your child.

But don't forget the importance of introducing your child to the world of nonfiction. The ability to read and comprehend factual material will be essential to your child in school, and throughout life. The Scholastic Science Readers™ series was created especially with beginning readers in mind. These books, with their clear texts and beautiful photographs, will help you to share the wonders of science with *your* new reader.

Suggested Activity

If you live near the ocean, you might have a chance to take a whale-watching cruise. You might even be lucky enough to spot dolphins from the shore. But for most people, the best place to see ocean creatures is at an aquarium. There are too many wonderful aquariums to list them all here. Check the phone book for an aquarium near you!

Aquarium visitors may safely watch sharks swim in their tanks, and observe lots of other sea life, too. Some aquariums have special exhibits that allow visitors to touch stingrays, sea stars, and other creatures. If there is no aquarium in your area, the Monterey Bay Aquarium's website will put you in touch with the watery world of the ocean. Try: **http://www.mbayaq.org/**